I0902231

IMAGES
of America

Hot Rodding in the San Fernando Valley

Members of the Road Kings of Burbank pensively view the newly completed club dragster on the night before its first race. The Road Kings combined showmanship, skill, and technical innovation to become perhaps the most successful car club in history, contributing more professional drivers and national champions than any other club on record. (Courtesy of Bob Muravez.)

On the Cover: Bob Muravez of the Road Kings car club is pictured at San Fernando drag strip driving the "Freight Train" championship-winning dragster. (Courtesy of Tom Jandt.)

IMAGES
of America

Hot Rodding in the San Fernando Valley

Tony Baker

ARCADIA
PUBLISHING

ISBN 978-1-4671-6065-0

Published by Arcadia Publishing
Charleston, South Carolina

Printed in the United States of America

Library of Congress Control Number: 2024932415

For all general information, please contact Arcadia Publishing:
Telephone 843-853-2070
Fax 843-853-0044
E-mail sales@arcadiapublishing.com

Visit us on the Internet at www.arcadiapublishing.com

Dedicated to Rod Pepmuller and Richard Martinez

Contents

ACKNOWLEDGMENTS

I'd like to thank the Road Kings of Burbank, and especially members Jim Miles, Tom Jandt, Tommy Ivo, Don Prudhomme, Butch Cederquist, Don Hoffman, Bob Muravez, Don Gaide, and Dick Plamondon, for contributing the images in this book and for their assistance and cooperation in putting the story together. Thanks also to Don Baldaseroni of the Burbank Historical Society, Bonneville historian Mark Lingua, and Jim Campbell for their help. Thanks to Desiree Gonzales for help with editorial matters and Dexter's Camera of Ventura for image processing. And finally, a big thank-you to my old friend Harry Mishkin; Adam, Tiffanie, and Josh at The Grape House of Jazz and Spirits; Tina van Curan at Autobooks/Aerobooks of Burbank; and the hot rod community of Southern California for all the support and encouragement that they've given me over the years.

Introduction

Originating in the United States, the culture of hot rodding has become a worldwide phenomenon. Clubs and individuals in the United Kingdom, Europe, Australia, South America, and elsewhere dedicate themselves to recreating classic American-style hot rods. Many of these enthusiasts received their first exposure to hot rodding by watching Hollywood-produced teenage exploitation movies like *Rebel Without a Cause*, *High School Confidential*, and *Hot Rod Gang*. Hollywood studios churned out a huge number of these films during the 1950s and 1960s, and with few exceptions, most were poorly acted melodramas about juvenile delinquents racing around in fast cars and getting in trouble of one kind or another. The real stars of these films were hot rods. Movie audiences were treated to images of kids in Model A roadsters, "deuce" coupes, and wild T-bucket hot rods tearing up the streets of Anytown, USA. The exteriors of these low-budget films were usually shot on the streets around the studios in Hollywood and the San Fernando Valley. These hot rods came from the car clubs.

The car club era in Southern California began in the late 1930s as groups of like-minded car enthusiasts gathered in various towns and cities. With names like the Throttlers and the Whistlers, groups of mostly young men represented their hometowns at timing association meets held in the desert northeast of Los Angeles with the object of seeing who had the fastest car. Club activities were interrupted by World War II but picked up again in the postwar period. Fueled by a strong economy and a growing population of young gearheads, the trend took off in the early 1950s.

By then, there were several dozen car clubs in the greater Los Angeles area, with many located in the San Fernando Valley. While some clubs were social in nature, dedicated to cruising and partying, others were more into cars and driving fast in the young and illicit motorsport of drag racing. One of the most illustrious was the Road Kings of Burbank, a club that started in the early days of the sport and did more to help drag racing attain worldwide popularity than any other club of the era. From the years 1952 to 1963, the Road Kings competed in every class that drag racing had to offer.

Burbank residents Jim Miles, Ralph Marshall, Dave Ostercamp, and Al Totleono, all in their early 20s, founded the Road Kings in November 1952. Marshall was the president, and the first meeting attracted 17 mostly teenage members. Dues were 25¢ a week. While not all the club members owned or even raced cars, all members participated in club racing activities, whether as drivers, mechanics, crew, or owners. Early on, the club began racing at Lou Baney's Saugus drag strip, one of the first in the area to stage legal quarter-mile drag races. The club raced a mixed handful of Fords and Chevrolets, some stock and some modified, all of them daily drivers. Founding member Jim Miles raced the 1941 Ford he drove to school each day. Tom Jandt, known as the "King of the River Road" for his success as a street racer, ran his highly modified Olds-powered 1932 coupe.

By 1954, some members of the club were building and racing cars that were set up solely for drag racing. Stripped-down coupes and roadsters specifically built for drag racing on asphalt had been around since the late 1940s and had features like a centered driver's position, relocated engine, and altered frame. The engines were all highly modified as well. Bored and stroked, supercharged, or with fuel injection, engines were seldom rated in horsepower in the early days but judged by how fast they made the car go.

Street racing, a popular illegal sport engaged in by almost all clubs, was done late at night on a long, straight, and deserted road that ran along the Los Angeles River just outside the Burbank city limits. Forest Lawn Drive, known to the club as the "Old River Road," was across the cement riverbed from the Warner Bros. and Disney studio lots. Isolated and little used in those days, it ran over a mile past a cemetery, some derelict movie sets, and into the back of Griffith Park. The Old River Road was the site of countless midnight street races throughout the 1950s and into the 1960s until encroaching real estate development and other factors put an end to it.

During this time, hot rod culture was beginning to take form, and while it was happening all over the country, it was particularly intense in Southern California and especially in the San Fernando Valley. By the mid-1950s, the valley was experiencing rapid growth in development and population. The population included an increasingly large percentage of teenagers who were attracted to the cool, reckless image that car clubs and hot rod culture offered. A few entrepreneurial hot rodders saw an opportunity and began staging legal races at some of the many abandoned former military airstrips that dotted the region.

The vast San Fernando Valley was a hotbed of hot rod activities, with the main action being east of Lankersheim Boulevard and west of Van Nuys Boulevard. The east side, dominated by the Road Kings, boasted the landmark Bob's Big Boy drive-in and racing on the Old River Road and was home to Barris Custom, Navarro Speed, Weiand, and Magic Muffler (which we will hear more about later). The tracts west of Lankersheim were populated by clubs like the Barons and the Ghost Riders. A deserted stretch of Chandler Boulevard was often the late-night venue for impromptu drag races. Farther west was Van Nuys Boulevard, which ran for several miles across the Valley from south to north and was a well-known cruise night destination. In the neighborhoods around the south end were the shops of Tony Nancy, Kent Fuller, Ed Pink, and Bud Ekin's legendary Triumph motorcycle dealership, a hangout of actor Steve McQueen. Where Van Nuys Boulevard crossed Victory Boulevard to the north in the domain of the Jesters car club was Van Nuys High School, which had the distinction of having its own on-campus drag strip. Nearby, on Sherman Way, was the B&M Hydro transmission shop, Zeuschel Racing Engines, and Roy Fjastad's Speed Shop. These are all just a few of the car clubs and hot rod–related businesses in the Valley that made it a cauldron of activity and innovation.

One

Kings of the Valley

The city of Burbank, in the east San Fernando Valley, was and still is the home turf of the Road Kings, and this image shows it as it was in the early 1950s. Dominating the center is the Warner Bros. Studios lot, bordered on the right by the concrete channel of the Los Angeles River. Running alongside the river to its right is Forest Lawn Drive, locally known as the Old River Road and the scene of many a late-night drag race. In the foreground is the community of Toluca Lake, where stars like Frank Sinatra and Bob Hope had their mansions. (Burbank Historical Society.)

Jim Miles, pictured here, was a founding member of the Road Kings. When Miles graduated high school in 1952, there were more than 60 car clubs in the San Fernando Valley. Not having a club in his neighborhood, Miles got together with another local hot rodder, Ralph Marshall, and started the Road Kings. The first meeting was on November 17, 1952. (Jim Miles.)

In 1955, Miles bought a 1934 Ford three-window coupe. He installed a Chrysler engine, initially running it on gasoline. Getting mediocre results from this setup, he replaced the carbs with a 671 blower and went back to running as a fueler. In this configuration, Miles raced the coupe until 1959, attaining speeds in the 150–155 mile-per-hour range with elapsed times in the quarter mile averaging 9.95 to 10.1 seconds. In this image from 1959, the Ford sports a bright red paint job. (Jim Miles.)

A few weeks after the club was formed, a friend took Miles to see the drag races at the newly opened Saugus drag strip, and Miles was hooked on the sport. Over the next two years, he raced various old Ford sedans, settling on the stripped-down 1941 Ford Tudor seen here. Note the holes visible at the back of the front and rear fenders. Miles built a flathead engine for the car and was routinely beaten by guys running Cadillac or Oldsmobile overheads in their cars. He eventually built a carbureted Chrysler engine for it and, running on fuel, got the sedan up to 119 miles per hour at Saugus. (Jim Miles.)

This is a snapshot of the strip at Saugus that Jim took on his first visit, taken from just ahead of the starting line. The staging and pit area was located to the left of the image. Set in a small valley among rolling hills, the former landing strip had no permanent infrastructure like a timing tower or concession stand. Instead, cokes, ice cream, and hot dogs were sold out of a cooler under the shade of an oak tree. (Jim Miles.)

The '34 was raced by Miles until mid-1959, with him trying different fuel system configurations and engines, gradually refining the coupe as he went along. Attaining speeds in the 150–155 mile-per-hour range with elapsed times in the quarter mile averaging 9.95 to 10.1 seconds, the steel-bodied car was competitive but too heavy. By the time these images were taken in 1959, Jim had the '34 painted a hot red color. Miles stands at center facing the camera in the image below. (Both, Jim Miles.)

Miles removed the engine and sold the car for $300. It was stolen from its new owner a few weeks later and disappeared. Many years later, it was discovered in a body shop in Sun Valley when someone there was watching a bodyman sanding old paint off the doors. The old Magic Muffler logo began to appear from under the paint, and it became apparent that this was the Jim Miles car. It has been restored to its original configuration. (Jim Miles.)

In 1960, Jim Miles built and drove what became one of the most famous fuel-altered cars, the Magic Muffler Fiat. Taking the fuel Chrysler engine from his '34, he installed it in a Scotty Fenn–built chassis for an altered. Miles decided to use a Fiat Topolino body for the altered and went on a search that took him all over Southern California. Finally finding an original steel Fiat body just a few blocks from his home in Burbank, Miles set to work. He stripped the body and painted it with a silver metallic undercoat. Next, multiple layers of violet tinting toner were applied by hand. The result was a deep, rich violet-blue color. The new dragster is seen here in the pits at Long Beach. (Jim Miles.)

Here it is in the pits at San Fernando. Jim raced the car in AA/altered class, which means it could be run with unlimited modifications, as opposed to a stock racer. The AA prefix referred to engine size and wheelbase. (Jim Miles.)

AA/altereds were beginning to rise in popularity with drag racing fans, as the full grandstands at left in this image show. In classic action, Jim Miles takes on Howard Cross in his Chevrolet-powered Fiat at Ramona some time in the early 1960s. (Jim Miles.)

The year is 1962. Miles relaxes with a cool beverage in his garage at home in Burbank after a day of drag racing. Hanging at left is his Deist fireproof racing suit. Deist, which is still based in Los Angeles, manufactures all types of safety equipment for motorsports. It also made the drag chute visible on the back of the Fiat. The use of parachutes to slow down a dragster at the end of a race was another innovation that came into being in the late 1950s as the speed of dragsters increased. (Jim Miles.)

Jim Miles's Fiat was destroyed during a hair-raising crash in 1964 when he rolled it going 171 miles per hour at the old Ramona drag strip on Paradise Mesa in San Diego County. Still sponsored by Magic Muffler, he quickly built another Fiat-bodied altered, shown here. The new altered was similar to the first one. Miles even used the same Chrysler engine, which had survived the crash at Ramona. The biggest difference was the fiberglass body of the new car, making it much lighter. While improving the top speed, the weight reduction made the Fiat's handling an even bigger challenge than before. (Jim Miles.)

Miles raced the car in this form from 1966 to 1968, and in that time, the little lavender-painted altered became an icon in western drag racing and was representative of the "Kandy Colored" pop culture that dominated the scene in Southern California at the time. Later on, it became noticeable that the cockpit of the fiberglass Fiat body had negative air pressure issues, so Jim later replaced it with a 1932 Bantam body. The car was finally wrecked when a novice driver was allowed to take it on a licensing run and it went airborne. (Jim Miles.)

Jim Miles's final venture into professional drag racing was with this fiberglass Model T–bodied altered named "Black Magic." Chassis builder George Brittig fabricated a funny car–style frame with a 125-inch wheelbase for better handling. Motive power was provided by a 392 Chrysler. Miles and his team raced Black Magic for seven years, campaigning all over the West. Miles had more or less stopped driving after his wreck at Ramona and was letting others drive his cars. Magic Muffler's sponsorship had begun to diminish as the chain's business began to fade out in the 1970s. Black Magic was wrecked in 1977 when a defective wheel failed at 220 miles per hour. The driver was seriously injured, and Miles decided that it was time to get out of racing altogether. (Jim Miles.)

Rod Pepmuller, pictured here, was a standout member of the Road Kings back in the mid-1950s. A popular, talented mechanic and welder, Pepmuller was employed at the Mobil gas station owned by Tom Jandt's father. Pepmuller served as part of the pit crew and often drove as well. Pepmuller and Jandt, along with Jim Miles, built the club roadster. Pepmuller later designed and built the frame for the club's rail dragster, which proved so successful that Pepmuller went into business building frames for other racers. Pepmuller would go on to operate his own garage in Burbank, R&R Automotive. By the late 1960s, Pepmuller had joined the growing drag boat movement, powering his boats with a succession of ever larger big-block Chrysler Hemi engines. He pursued the sport right up until the mid-1990s, when failing health forced his retirement. (Tom Jandt.)

One of the early star drivers in the Road Kings was Tom Jandt. Joining the Road Kings in 1953, Jandt quickly became known for having the fastest hot rod in Burbank. He is seen here posing with his 1932 Ford. Jandt bought the engineless coupe, installed an Olds Rocket V8 from a junkyard, and went racing. He was known as the "King of the Old River Road." (Tom Jandt.)

By the age of 15, Tom Jandt had saved enough money from delivering newspapers to buy this 1940 Ford Tudor sedan. He painted it metallic blue and installed a Model A leaf spring over the rear axle to raise it up. This did not improve the handling any but did attract attention on cruise nights. (Tom Jandt.)

Tom Jandt's 1932 Ford deuce coupe (deuce indicating the "2" in the year 1932) is seen here. Powered by a 410-cubic-inch Oldsmobile engine, Jandt's coupe was the scourge of such legendary early drag strips like San Fernando, Pomona, Bakersfield, and Saugus. This view shows the many trophies won by Jandt and the coupe at races across the Southland. (Tom Jandt.)

Here is a good profile view of Tom Jandt's coupe, parked at his dad's Mobil station on Olive Avenue. Tom painted the car at the body shop visible in the left background, where he had a part-time job. The sealed-beam headlights were after-market units. (Tom Jandt.)

For a short time, Jandt fitted a Scott blower on the Olds, shown here. It was not a successful arrangement, however, and he returned to using four, and later six, single-barrel Stromberg carburetors on a custom manifold. (Tom Jandt.)

The full-fendered coupe was painted pale yellow with white steel wheels. The seats and door cards were upholstered with tan leather, a step up from the more common vinyl. Note the "baby" moon hub cap up front. Hanging from the rear-view mirror are a pair of fuzzy dice. (Tom Jandt.)

As hot rods go, Tom Jandt's coupe was fairly clean and simple in appearance. Except for the addition of 1951 Chevrolet taillights, little has been done to modify the body. The valve covers of the Olds engine peeking out from under the hood and the exhaust cut-off going through the fender betray the hot rod's true nature. (Tom Jandt.)

In May 1955, Tom Jandt had the fastest track time in the Southern California National Championship, held at San Fernando drag strip. Besides a trophy, the winner got his picture taken with the trophy girl, movie and television actress Carolyn Craig. (Tom Jandt.)

Carolyn Craig poses with Tom Jandt's coupe. Jandt, like others in the club, would rent the car to movie studios for use as props in teenage exploitation films, usually earning around $25, big money in the 1950s. The coupe can be seen briefly in the movie *Hot Rod Girl* in scenes shot at San Fernando drag strip. (Tom Jandt.)

Tom Jandt's coupe raced in the "B" gas class. The lettering on the cowl says, "Road Kings No. 3," a reference to Jandt's status as a driver in the club, with Tommy Ivo and Don Prudhomme holding the first and second slots. The headlights were frequently removed for racing. Note the holes drilled in the dropped axle. (Tom Jandt.)

Tom Jandt's 410-cubic-inch Oldsmobile Rocket V8, seen here set up with four carbs, was fitted with Howard cams. This engine would later be installed in the Road Kings club dragster. Power was transferred to the rear wheels through a LaSalle transmission. A plentiful supply of complete overhead V8s like the Rocket could be found in junkyards for around $50. Combined with the LaSalle trans and 4.11 gears in the rear end and six carbs, Jandt's coupe could get to 113 miles per hour in a quarter mile. (Tom Jandt.)

Scenes like the one in this image were common on the residential blocks east of the Warner lot. A group of young men are gathered around what appears to be some engine parts, engaged in deep conversation on a warm early afternoon in Burbank. The new-looking Ford Mainline Tudor parked in the background dates the image to around 1953, and the Verdugo Mountains are just visible through the haze in the left background. (Tom Jandt.)

Tom Jandt's coupe is seen here on the starting line just prior to a qualifying run at San Fernando. Before competing in a National Hot Rod Association (NHRA)–sanctioned race, cars had to show they could meet minimum speeds. In the background is a 1953 Ford Crestline Victoria hardtop coupe. (Tom Jandt.)

The automotive shop class at John Burroughs High School, seen here in the background, gave Road King members a place to hone their mechanical skills. Tom Jandt is standing at center with three unidentified classmates. (Tom Jandt.)

Arthur's Drive-In, located in Burbank at the intersection of Victory Boulevard and Olive Avenue, was one of many cruise night destinations for clubs like the Road Kings, although their main hangout was the famous Bob's Big Boy in Toluca Lake. (Burbank Historical Society.)

Club member Gary Jolly owned this neat little 1931 Ford roadster. This image was taken in the alley behind Tom Jandt's parents' house on Brighton Street in Burbank. Paul Stewart is second from the right. Tom is standing on the right. Tom's Olds is in the engine bay. (Tom Jandt.)

Seen in action at San Fernando in 1955, Tom Jandt and the coupe are shutting down a 1939 Ford. The Oldsmobile engine in Tom's car ran on pump gasoline, as opposed to the fuel-class dragsters, which ran on exotic fuel mixes based on nitromethane and alcohol. (Tom Jandt.)

The 410-cubic-inch Oldsmobile Rocket V8 was quite an engine in its day. Jandt preferred to use the readily available and affordable Stromberg 97 carburetor. The fuel system was pressurized for races with an old-fashioned hand pump mounted on the dashboard in lieu of a fuel pump. (Tom Jandt.)

Tom Jandt grins as he stands by his mount after a day's racing. Throughout 1955 and 1956, Jandt dominated the region's drag strips in this car. Note the exhaust stains on the lower left of the driver's door, caused by bypassing the car's street exhaust system. (Tom Jandt.)

After a successful career terrorizing the local drag strips, the '32 sits behind the Mobil station with a "For Sale" sign in the window. By this time, it has acquired a set of full moon hubcaps. Like most hot rods of the era, it disappeared soon after. (Tom Jandt.)

Tom Jandt then moved on to this 1940 Ford coupe, pictured in front of his parents' house on Brighton Street in Burbank. One of the best-looking cars ever built, the 1940 model is highly sought by collectors. The bumpers and hubcaps have already been removed for racing. (Tom Jandt.)

Jandt removed the Olds engine from the '32 before selling it and installed it in this car. Equipped with a Paxton blower and an early B&M Hydromatic transmission, the combination managed a respectable elapsed time of 14.64 seconds in the quarter mile, crossing the line at 108.69 miles per hour at San Fernando in December 1958. (Tom Jandt.)

For dates or cruising, Tom Jandt's ride was this 1955 Ford Thunderbird. Tom made the short drive over the hill to Hollywood to have renowned artist Von Dutch apply the pinstripes over the stock red paint. Note the white sidewall tires and a set of Kelsey-Hayes wire wheels. (Tom Jandt.)

More of a personal luxury car than a sports car, the Thunderbird was Ford's more refined answer to the Chevrolet Corvette. Outselling the Corvette at a ratio of 24 to 1 when introduced in 1955, the Thunderbird came equipped with a 283-cubic-inch V8 compared to the anemic six-cylinder powering the Corvette. (Tom Jandt.)

Another important early member of the Road Kings was Butch Cederquist. Butch and his older brother Dave were originally members of the North Hollywood–Van Nuys–based Road Rumblers car club. In late 1953, the Road Kings recruited Dave and Butch, already experienced drag racers, into their club. The brothers joined up, and Butch began a 10-year-long stint as a driver, finishing up in 1963 as junior top eliminator. (Butch Cederquist.)

While attending Van Nuys High School, Butch used this 1940 Ford as his daily driver, which he also would take out on the strip at San Fernando. The flathead-powered red coupe could make 89–90 miles per hour at the drags. (Butch Cederquist.)

The Cederquist brothers got their start in drag racing with Dave's white 1929 Ford Model A hot rod, seen here parked in their parents' driveway in the spring of 1955. Dave drove the car to school before turning it into a drag racer. It went through a variety of engines, at first a flathead, which was soon replaced by a Dodge overhead. (Butch Cederquist.)

After about a year and a lot of work, the roadster had acquired a coat of red paint, a roll bar, another engine (this time, a DeSoto), and a lot of trophies. Note the motorcycle fenders and interesting front Nerf bar/ license plate holder. (Butch Cederquist.)

This image shows a Chrysler Hemi installed in the street hot rod turned drag racer. The engine has four Stromberg 97 carbs on the intake manifold, and the exhaust is handled by chrome-tipped headers. With the Chrysler, the car ran at 115 miles per hour. (Butch Cederquist.)

During an early race at Pomona drag strip in the spring of 1955, strip officials turned the brothers away because they showed up at the strip without a hood, which was required equipment for racing there. Butch and Dave Cederquist responded by removing a piece of corrugated metal from a nearby outbuilding, cutting it to shape, and attaching it to their car. (Butch Cederquist.)

Late one afternoon in July 1957 at Saugus drag strip, Road Kings Tom Jandt and Larry Sutton (facing camera) found themselves without enough gasoline in Sutton's car to get back to Burbank, a considerable drive. They got caught on camera "borrowing" a few gallons from an unwitting friend. (Courtesy of Don Hoffman.)

After taking Dave Cederquist's hot rod as far as it would go performance-wise, the brothers put together a car meant solely for drag racing. Mounting a steel 1929 Ford roadster body on 1932 frame rails, the Cederquists put a carbureted Chrysler Hemi in the engine bay. Clay Smith supplied the camshafts free of charge, something it did for many up-and-coming drag racers, and a large sticker of the company's logo adorns the cowl. The wire wheels up front came from a 1932 Harley-Davidson motorcycle and were supplied by club founder Jim Miles. (Butch Cederquist.)

The well-finished Cederquist dragster is a good example of the type of car that ran in the mid- to late 1950s. Older steel-bodied dragsters still largely based on stock automobiles like Dave Cederquist's soon evolved into the tube frame and fiberglass-bodied custom-built cars that were drag racing by the start of the 1960s. (Butch Cederquist.)

A frontal view of the Cederquist dragster shows the Hemi engine visible through the 1932 radiator shell. Since the engine had to run for only a quarter mile, overheating was not a big problem, and radiators were considered to add unnecessary weight. (Butch Cederquist.)

This is a rear-angle view of the dragster seen parked next to the Cederquist home on Kitteridge Avenue in North Hollywood. Note the vented trunk lid and Road Kinks plaque. That is a 1932 radiator shell on the well-finished maroon-painted steel body. (Butch Cederquist.)

The Cederquist dragster is pictured on its trailer at San Fernando. By 1956, Butch was using the race number 52. He had originally wanted to race using the number 25, but that was already in use by many others, including Art Chrisman, so he used the reverse. Standing at right wearing glasses is Bernie Partridge of the Dust Devils car club and manager of the drag strip at Inyokern. (Butch Cederquist.)

In this image, Butch Cederquist, in the foreground, leaves the starting line at San Fernando in a race against Bart Chinchero. The Cederquist brothers and Chinchero had an informal rivalry at the drag strip, with the brothers taking top eliminator one week and Chinchero the next. (Butch Cederquist.)

Butch Cederquist sits up in the cockpit of the dragster as he is pushed down the return road after a race at San Fernando. Note the hay bales in the background, which were used as a barrier along the drag strip. Butch's 1957 Chevrolet Nomad is being used as the push car. (Butch Cederquist.)

Cederquist entered the wild world of AA/fuel-altered drag racing in this Bantam-bodied roadster. Seen here in its early alcohol-fuel configuration, the roadster was built by Ed Wedel and featured an alcohol-fueled 392 Hemi equipped with "barn door" Enderly fuel injection. The fiberglass body is from Kurt Hamilton of Cal Automotive. (Butch Cederquist.)

Here is the altered after its conversion to nitro fuel in 1961. Running on nitro, the roadster turned 171 miles per hour at the strip and held the number-one spot as junior top eliminator. Here, it leaves a cloud of burning rubber and nitro fuel fumes in front of a sparse crowd at Lyons drag strip. (Butch Cederquist.)

Up until around 1954, the members of the Road Kings raced their personal cars at the local drag strips. Tom Jandt and Rod Pepmuller, along with Jim Miles, combined some odd parts they had lying around their garages and built this neat little roadster for club members to use. The three exhaust pipes indicate that there is a flathead in the engine bay. (Tom Jandt.)

The dragster was shared by the club members, who would install their own engines when they wanted to race. First in was Jandt's Oldsmobile, and then Jim Miles's 3/8-by-3/8 AB flathead was in it when he raced the car. (Tom Jandt.)

The initiation of a new member into the club usually involved putting him into some type of embarrassing situation, like going out in public dressed in outlandish costumes. Tommy Ivo, a diabolical and notorious prankster, was in charge of the initiation rites. This shot was taken in June 1957. (Tom Jandt.)

The flat, concrete-lined channel that is the Los Angeles River is practically dry most of the year and was a convenient place for members of the Road Kings to test their cars since most of them lived nearby. Here, a group works on the engine of Jim Miles's 1934 coupe in the shade of an overpass. (Tom Jandt.)

With the experience of building the club roadster under their belts, Tom Jandt and Rod Pepmuller moved on to something more ambitious. The result was the dragster pictured here, with a chassis built by Pepmuller and powered by Jandt's trusty Oldsmobile. Sometimes called the "Gold Dragster," it was state of the art for the time. (Tom Jandt.)

This shot of Pepmuller behind the wheel was taken at Taft, California, in May 1958. The flagman has just dropped the green flag as the dragster's front wheels can be seen just leaving the ground. "Popping a wheelie" was a sure way to please the crowd at a drag race. (Tom Jandt.)

The bigger, more powerful engines used in the new cars required a stronger chassis made of welded chromoly steel tubing, or "aircraft tube," as it was called. Features like safety harnesses and shields to protect the driver from exploding transmissions were developed more from experience than NHRA regulation. (Tom Jandt.)

The Pepmuller and Jandt dragster frame is seen here while under construction in Rod Pepmuller's garage in Burbank. Tom Jandt's engineless coupe sits next to it. Note Jandt's Oldsmobile engine sitting on the floor under the workbench in the background. (Tom Jandt.)

This image shows the dragster's rear end to good advantage. The body is gold-painted 16-gauge aluminum cut to shape and attached to the frame with sheet metal screws. Just visible at the far right are the hand pump and pressure gauges for the compressed-air fuel system. Note the chrome metal trim strip above the club plaque. (Tom Jandt.)

This is the Pepmuller and Jandt dragster on the first day it raced at San Fernando in May 1958. During the late 1950s, rail dragsters transitioned from the crude machines that were seen just a few years earlier. Gone were the days of chassis fabricated from plumbers' pipe and angle iron powered by flathead engines. (Tom Jandt.)

Rod built a second chassis with a little more room for the driver. Here, it is stripped of engine and bodywork. Like many an early designer, Pepmuller drew the outline of the frame on the floor using chalk and a tape measure, going largely by what looked right. The chromoly tubing was cut to length and welded, which required a special technique that only skilled welders like Pepmuller possessed. (Tom Jandt.)

As the flagman looks on, Tom Jandt lifts off from the strip at Bakersfield during the early summer of 1958. The heavy steel truck wheels used on the dragster's early races have been replaced with lighter, more aesthetically pleasing wire motorcycle wheels. (Tom Jandt.)

Pepmuller and Jandt towed the dragster to the races on this old-fashioned single-axle trailer behind Rod's 1951 Ford. Note the 16-inch steel truck wheels and full moon hubcaps mounted on the front. This image was taken in the driveway of Rod's house in Burbank in June 1958. (Tom Jandt.)

The next engine in the Pepmuller and Jandt dragster was Jim Miles's blown Chrysler Hemi. This image was taken after a race when a piece of the supercharger duct blew off during an engine backfire with Tom Jandt behind the wheel. (Tom Jandt.)

After a race, drivers and crew would hang out in an area near the end of the drag strip at San Fernando. Seen from left to right are Ronny Rayburn (in white shirt), Jim Miles leaning over the engine, Rod Pepmuller (in short sleeve shirt looking down), and two unidentified individuals. (Tom Jandt.)

Older luxury sedans a bit past their prime have always been a popular choice for late-night cruising. Tom Jandt's younger brother Jerry bought this beautiful 1938 Packard Twelve seven-passenger limousine from the nuns at the Villa Cabrini convent in Burbank. Standing from left to right are Tom's father, his younger brother Jerry, and Tom. (Tom Jandt.)

Jerry Jandt also owned this very nice 1951 Cadillac Series 62 Coupe de Ville hardtop. Jerry sanded and sprayed the body with white lacquer in the garage of his dad's service station. Afterward, the particulate residue in the air from the spraying settled on all the surfaces inside the garage, covering everything with a coat of white lacquer. (Tom Jandt.)

For fun, Tom Jandt built this miniature version of the club dragster. Using the engine, transmission, and differential taken from a 1934 Crosley, the mini dragster always put on a good show for the spectators. (Tom Jandt.)

Here is a good view of the Pepmuller and Jandt dragster's unique front suspension setup. Designed and fabricated by Rod Pepmuller, it consisted of a single antifriction shock attached to the center front of the chassis. The star-shaped knob visible at center was for adjusting the stiffness of the shock. This was attached to a 1939 Ford tubular front axle by way of adjustable linkages on either side of the center. Tracking was handled by turnbuckle-style linkages connecting the corners of the chassis to each end of the axle. According to Tom Jandt, the setup was successful; the dragster ran straight and true, with good ride and handling characteristics. (Tom Jandt.)

In 1962, Tom Jandt assembled this rail using a Scotty Fenn chassis. Kent Enderley built the Ardun-Ford V8. Equipped with a Scott blower and Enderley fuel injection, the dragster ran speeds in the neighborhood of 140 miles per hour but would suffer rocker-arm failure often. The Ardun overhead conversion kits for the Ford flathead engine were expensive and heavy, weighing in at 60 pounds. Nonetheless, they were a popular way of improving performance, offering an increase of power from 25 to 60 percent, depending on tuning. (Tom Jandt.)

Tom Jandt dropped an Oldsmobile engine fitted with a Paxton blower along with a B&M automatic transmission into this 1940 Ford coupe and went racing. The image below shows Tom poised on the starting line ready to go up against a black 1959 Corvette just before the starter drops his flag. Note the hay bales used as the strip's boundary fence. This would soon be replaced by a sturdier version of chain-link covered by advertising signs. (Both, Tom Jandt.)

This mildly customized 1959 Chevrolet El Camino belongs to Bob Muravez. Pictured at Famoso drag strip in Bakersfield, Muravez has replaced the stock grill with chrome strips. The 1959 El Camino pickup came with a 283-cubic-inch V8, although a 348-cubic-inch engine with a potential horsepower rating of 315 was available as an option. (Tom Jandt.)

The late 1950s were a period of experimentation and innovation in the technology of drag racing. Ideas for improving performance were tried out, copied, and improved upon at the drag strips as the different clubs met each week at the strip. This photograph was taken at Pomona during the early summer of 1958. (Tom Jandt.)

These images, taken shortly after Tom installed the Olds engine in his 1940 coupe, show his friends and classmates from high school gathered together discussing and commenting upon his work. John Lieberneck stands at center with his arms crossed, and Gary Jolly is in the white T-shirt at the left. (Both, Tom Jandt.)

The massive Warner Bros. Studios lot dominated the west side of the small town of Burbank, with the even larger Universal Studios and backlot just to the east across the Los Angeles River. Tom's 1947 Ford Tudor is seen parked on Olive Avenue across from the Warner sound stages. (Tom Jandt.)

Tom Jandt's "daily driver" for a time was this mild custom 1950 Ford Deluxe Tudor sedan. Seen parked in the lot of his father's gas station across from the Warner Bros. Studios, Jandt dropped yet another Oldsmobile engine in it and painted the car lemon yellow. (Tom Jandt.)

This is a good view of the second club dragster. The biggest difference between the first and second dragster was that the chassis on the second car had a wider frame around the driver and a trapeze-style roll bar. The cockpit was skinned with an unpainted aluminum sheet. In this shot, the dragster is powered by a Chrysler Hemi with six carbs. (Tom Jandt.)

Tom Jandt (center) is seen here doing a field adjustment on the club dragster's rear axle as members of the crew offer advice. The location appears to be the infield at Pomona. Note the air intakes on Jandt's Hemi. (Tom Jandt.)

Club members Owen Engle (at left) and Kent Baber (leaning on the roll bar) put together this interesting rail dragster. The engine is a Model A Ford AB four-cylinder converted to an overhead and mounting three Stromberg carburetors. Baber was the driver. (Tom Jandt.)

Tom Jandt's last run in the second dragster was at San Fernando. The lower-end bearings failed at the end of the run and dropped the crankshaft onto the pavement. The dragster spun out and wound up pointing the wrong way on the drag strip, leaving a large puddle of engine fluids. (Tom Jandt.)

After the engine was destroyed at San Fernando, Jandt sold the dragster to club members Bob Muravez and Don Gaide. Muravez and Gaide took the rail back to the drag strip after installing a blown gas Chevrolet engine. Muravez's El Camino pickup is being used as a push car. (Tom Jandt.)

Burbank High School student Brent Chinchero drove this 1932 roadster, seen here parked at the Jandt Mobil station. The full-fendered hot rod was powered by a fuel-injected Cadillac. The windshield has been removed and equipped with racing slicks and a roll bar, and the maroon and black roadster looks ready to race. (Tom Jandt.)

Tom Jandt's dad, Harry, operated a gas station for the Richfield Oil Company on Olive Avenue for many years. Located almost directly across the street from the Warner Bros. Studios' main gate, the station was typical of the spotlessly clean and well-run service stations of the era. Harry Jandt would later be lured away from Richfield to operate a station that Mobil was building next door on Olive Avenue. This also proved to be successful and operated for many years. Today, the site is occupied by a parking structure. (Both, Tom Jandt.)

Flashing a toothy grin, "TV" Tommy Ivo smiles for the camera. One of the Road Kings' most illustrious members, Ivo was a former child actor in Hollywood who had successfully transitioned into young adult roles and was making a good enough income in movies and television to indulge in his passion for cars in general and driving them fast in particular. A resident of Burbank and a student at Burroughs High School (class of 1954), Ivo was introduced to drag racing by Tom Jandt, who took him to see his first race at Saugus and sponsored his membership in the Road Kings. Ivo quickly became one of the club's star drivers. (Tom Jandt.)

Tommy Ivo's income as an actor enabled him to buy his first car at the age of 16. After looking over different car manufacturers' brochures with his girlfriend, he decided that he liked the looks of Buicks. He then walked into a Buick dealer with $3,000 and bought the new 1952 Buick Super seen here. (Tommy Ivo Collection.)

The Buick had a rather disappointing performance when Ivo took it racing at San Fernando with Tom Jandt, so he turned the car into this eye-catching custom. Ivo did all the work himself, a habit he followed with virtually every car he owned and raced thereafter. (Tommy Ivo Collection.)

Ivo's next car was a brand new 1955 Buick Century, powered by a 322-cubic-inch, 236-horsepower "Nailhead" V8 engine. This was an improvement over the anemic inline eight that was in his first car, and Ivo wasted no time in chroming and polishing everything he could in the engine bay. The stock 1955 Buicks were quick, and Ivo demonstrated this by winning top eliminator in his class the first time he raced the car at Saugus. (Tommy Ivo Collection.)

Tommy Ivo's success in this first day of racing aroused the suspicions of one of his competitors, who lodged a complaint with Lou Baney, the man who ran the show at Saugus. Baney took one look at all the chrome under the hood and mistakenly accused Ivo of illegally modifying the stock engine. Ivo's sarcastic answer to Baney led to his expulsion from the strip, an unfortunate event that would often repeat itself at other strips around the Southland. (Tommy Ivo Collection.)

Tommy Ivo's next car, the one that established his reputation as a skilled designer and builder of hot rods and dragsters, was his famous "bucket" Model T, pictured here. After seeing Norm Grabowski's trend-setting "kookie" Model T one cruise night at the drive-in at Toluca Lake, Ivo wanted to build one of his own. After carefully inspecting Grabowski's machine and taking a few measurements, Ivo set out to build his own. He found the body of a derelict Model T touring car in the desert wastes an hour's drive north of Burbank, and using a Model A frame, he had the basis for a hot rod. (Tommy Ivo Collection.)

A raked Model T roadster body, a big engine, lots of chrome, and a bright metallic paint job are all common features of the average T-bucket. Cars like Ivo's and Grabowski's were at home on the drag strip and could be driven on the street as well. But as the trend wore on, T-buckets became more and more outlandish in design and evolved into being strictly show cars. (Tommy Ivo Collection.)

Already a confirmed Buick fan, Ivo chose Buick's overhead-valve Fireball V8 to power the hot rod. Nicknamed the "Nailhead" because the exhaust valves were so small that they resembled nails, the 1955 model engines were 322 cubic inches in size and produced up to 255 horsepower. Tommy used this six-carb setup. (Tommy Ivo Collection.)

Tommy Ivo cut the four-door convertible body of the touring car in two to make a two-door roadster and grafted a shortened Model T pickup bed onto that. Note the meticulous attention to detail around the rear axle and license plate mounting. The candy-apple-red paint has been accented with pin-stripping by Von Dutch. (Tommy Ivo Collection.)

When Ivo took his roadster to the strip, the lightweight, powerful little hot rod became the scourge of the Southern California drag racing scene. Winning "best of class" on virtually every outing led to resentment among certain competitors of Ivo's, who believed that a car as good-looking as Ivo's was could not also be so fast without having some illegal modifications made to it. They would protest to strip officials, and Ivo's car would have to undergo an inspection. In this shot taken at San Fernando, Ivo is about to race a 1932 roadster. (Tommy Ivo Collection.)

The fact that Ivo was already in the film business and lived near the studios made it easy to get the car into films. His success at this enterprise led to *Car Craft* magazine running an article in its August 1957 issue about how to get one's hot rod into the movies. Here he is with two models posing for the cover. (Tommy Ivo Collection.)

Here is Tommy Ivo at San Fernando about to take a victory run down the return lane with the trophy girl. Standing in the back from left to right are Road King members Richard Gates, Ron Van Netta, and Dale Nordstrum. Barnett Buick of Burbank was Ivo's local car dealer. (Tommy Ivo Collection.)

Tom Jandt took this image of Tommy Ivo and several Road Kings after a successful day of racing. From left to right are Ron Van Netta, Richard Gates, Tommy Ivo, Dale Nordstrum, Larry Sutton, and Ronny Rayburn. In 1956, when this image was taken, the Road Kings of Burbank were growing both in membership and in reputation as a club for serious drag racers. (Tommy Ivo Collection.)

As Tommy Ivo's T-bucket continued to win at the strip, the protests and scrutiny continued, and it got to the point where Ivo decided that racing the little hot rod was no longer worth the trouble. In 1956, he retired it from the strip, and for a while, he rented it out to the movie studios as a picture car, where it appeared in teenage exploitation films like *Drag Strip Girl* and *The Choppers.* Ivo eventually sold the hot rod, which underwent an ill-advised custom job by George Barris, who altered the appearance of the car. It has since been restored to its original configuration and paint scheme, down to the Von Dutch pin-stripping. (Tommy Ivo Collection.)

This is what Tommy Ivo called the "Hate" roadster. Tired of all the harassment he suffered from drag strip officials and the constant scrutineering of his immaculately turned-out T-bucket, he wanted a bit of revenge. His idea was to build the worst-looking, fastest roadster he could and take it to the strip. Using his highly modified Buick engine and a shabby assemblage of junkyard parts, Ivo built the creation shown here. Note the meat cleaver stuck into the trunk lid. He took it to Lyons drag strip, where he beat everyone and was then thrown out by drag strip manager Mickey Thompson. (Tom Jandt.)

Tommy Ivo's entry into the world of rail dragsters happened when Don "the Beachcomber" Johnson asked Ivo if he would install his Buick engine in Johnson's frame and be the driver. Ivo accepted and began his professional racing career. Known as the Daddy's Auto Body dragster, after the shop that sponsored it, the dragster's frame was fabricated by a young welder named Kent Fuller, who would build many other cars for Ivo and others over the years. (Tom Jandt.)

Here is Tommy Ivo hanging out after a race at San Fernando. Dissatisfied with both the performance of the Daddy's Auto Body dragster and his partnership with Johnson, Ivo decided to go solo and build the dragster seen here. He went to Kent Fuller for the frame and used his Buick racing engine for power. The lightweight dragster was incredibly quick for the time, consistently beating more powerful Hemi-powered cars. At Santa Ana, on August 17, 1958, Ivo broke the world's record for elapsed time in a quarter mile at 9.50 seconds. (Tom Jandt.)

Another actor and Burbank resident who was a member of the Road Kings was Skip Torgeson. A popular member of the club, Skip had done some supporting roles in films and television and was known as the owner of one of the great early hot rods, the Banto and Macchia Model T roadster, built in 1949 (seen here). While not really involved in racing, Torgeson's contribution to the sport was to introduce a friend named Don Prudhomme to Tommy Ivo one night at Bob's drive-in. (Tom Jandt.)

Ivo and Prudhomme formed an immediate friendship, and it was suggested to Prudhomme that he attend a Road Kings meeting. Prudhomme was a member of another valley club, the Chancellors, but was not really happy with the club and was ready to move on. One meeting with the Road Kings was all it took, and Prudhomme was a member. Here, he is on the very first drag race of his long career, behind the wheel of the club dragster at San Fernando. Rod Pepmuller is driving the Buick push car. (Tom Jandt.)

Throughout the summer of 1959, Don Prudhomme alternated with Rod Pepmuller as club driver at strips around Southern California and began to realize that he had a natural ability at the sport. Prudhomme was also a skilled auto body painter and began doing work for Tommy Ivo, who was building his twin-engine dragster. When Ivo's first dragster became surplus to his needs, he sold it to Prudhomme. In this image, Prudhomme (center right in dark jacket) talks to Ivo (center left) just before Prudhomme's first race in the dragster at San Fernando. (Tom Jandt.)

Twin-engine dragsters were becoming popular, and in 1960, Ivo joined the movement. Seen here at San Fernando, the new dragster was powered by two Buick engines and appears fairly conventional in this image. Don Prudhomme can be seen behind the dragster facing the cockpit. (Tom Jandt.)

The two Buick engines that powered the dragster were mounted side by side, sharing power through the flywheel starter gears. The layout was visually striking, with injector tubes and exhaust pipes sticking out at all angles. (Tom Jandt.)

Ivo reversed the direction of one engine so they would run in harmony, a technology first used in twin-engine speedboats to eliminate vibration. Kent Fuller built the 88-inch-wheelbase chassis with the same trapeze-style roll cage as was on Ivo's first dragster. (Tom Jandt.)

The two images on this page were taken during a photo shoot at Lyons drag strip as Tommy Ivo poses with a trophy girl. The "Monster," as the gas-powered dragster was known, quickly became the fastest car in the region, setting world records in speed and elapsed time. (Tom Jandt.)

With the success of the new dragster, Tommy Ivo booked a tour of drag strips across the country and asked his friend Don Prudhomme to accompany him as crew. The two set out on an adventure that would eventually lead to Ivo becoming a world-renowned showman and international ambassador for the sport of drag racing and Prudhomme, later known to all as "the Snake," becoming a giant in the world of Top Fuel drag racing and a successful businessman. If Tom Jandt had not introduced Ivo to the Road Kings and Skip Torgeson introduced Prudhomme to Ivo, American motorsports would likely be quite different than it is today. (Tom Jandt.)

By 1956, the Road Kings of Burbank had gained a reputation as the club for serious drag racers and continued to attract new members. Among them were two more residents of Burbank, Bob Muravez (standing left) and Don Gaide (right). Gaide bought the engineless Jandt-Pepmuller dragster from Rod Pepmuller and partnered with Muravez, who had a Chevrolet 283 engine. Here, they are seen in the garage of Gaide's parents' house right after acquiring the dragster. (Bob Muravez.)

Muravez is in the cockpit and Gaide stands in this staged shot taken at Lyons drag strip in the late 1950s. By now, the dragster had been given the nickname "Gray Ghost" because of its silver-gray paint scheme. The small-block Chevrolet engine was bored and stroked to 330 cubic inches and had a one-of-a-kind Enderly "barn door" fuel injection system mated to a very rare GM 3-71 supercharger. The BB/gas-class dragster's career ended at San Fernando while being driven by Gaide. Blinded when an ill-fitting borrowed helmet fell over his eyes, Gaide chose to steer the dragster straight into the dry wash at the end of the strip rather than hit a crowd of spectators that had gathered nearby. Gaide was unhurt, but the long-serving dragster was totaled. (Bob Muravez.)

Don Gaide next partnered with fellow Road King Ken Safford and business partner Don Ratican to race the car shown here. Rod Pepmuller built the distinctive high-back chassis, with Gaide and Ratican building the Olds engine. The Safford, Gaide, and Ratican team won 17 of its first 22 races in this car. (Don Gaide.)

Ken Safford treats the crowd at Long Beach drag strip to a big cloud of smoke in this 1963 image. Safford, Gaide, and Ratican were on fire during this period, winning three major races over New Year's weekend in 1963 and then becoming one of the few teams to defeat fellow Road King Don Prudhomme at Lyons drag strip in February 1964. They also set top speed for the meet at the 1964 Winternationals at Pomona. (Don Gaide.)

Don Gaide deploys his drag chute to slow down after a race at Fontana in 1960. The chute was manufactured by Deist, a company that had a long association with the Road Kings. The first prototype Deist drag chute was tested out on the club dragster when it was being run by Gaide and Bob Muravez. The Deist company still manufactures safety equipment in Los Angeles. (Don Gaide.)

Road King Ken Safford gets a little smoke off the rear wheels of the Safford, Gaide, and Rattigan dragster during a warm-up on the long-gone drag strip at San Gabriel. Note the board mounted to the front axle, used as a way to keep the dragster's nose down during the start of a race. (Don Gaide.)

These images from 1953 show Road King Don Hoffman's 1929 Model A in the pits of the drag strip at the Los Angeles County Fairgrounds in Pomona. Hoffman had to use a piece of scrap corrugated metal as a hood on his flathead-powered hot rod in order to meet equipment requirements at the strip, something that also happened to fellow Road King Butch Cederquist at the same strip. (Both, Don Hoffman.)

In this image from October 1957, Rod Pepmuller sits in the cockpit as club members push him toward the starting line. The four upswept exhaust pipes belong to Jandt's Olds engine. Pushing the car are Kent Baber (left, with his hand on the cowling), Tom Jandt (standing center), Larry Sutton (in the white T-shirt), and Paul Stuart (far right). The design of the Road Kings club roadster was more or less obsolete by the end of the 1950s, replaced by purpose-built rail dragsters as drag racing technology advanced. (Tom Jandt.)

Bob Muravez moved on to his next car, building a new Chevrolet engine, again with Enderly injection but with a more conventional 671 supercharger, and placing it in a Kent Fuller frame. In this shot taken at Fontana drag strip, Muravez is in the cockpit, and standing at left is Ken Stafford, who would become quite a successful driver on his own; Don Gaide is at center and Ed Janke is on the right. (Bob Muravez.)

Here, Bob Muravez and the dragster are seen at the end of the San Fernando strip right after a race. Note how the Fuller-built frame comes to a point where it attaches to the front axle, a feature Fuller discontinued in later builds. (Bob Muravez.)

In 1961, Bob Muravez started driving the Quincy Automotive Special for Nye Frank and John Peters, a talented pair of designer/mechanics who worked at Bill Cox's speed shop in Santa Monica. Standing from left to right are Nye Frank, an unidentified Pomona drag strip official, Bob Muravez, and John Peters. (Bob Muravez.)

Twin-engine dragsters were in vogue in 1961, and the "Quincy Special" was Frank and Peters's take on the concept. Bob Muravez and "the Special" were a good match, as seen here on March 10, 1962, when Muravez notched his first major championship by winning Top Gas at the Bakersfield Fuel and Gas Championship, more popularly known as the "March Meet." (Bob Muravez.)

In an attempt to improve the bite of the rear wheels into to road surface, Frank and Peters mounted rectangular plywood boards to the frame in order to direct air over the wheels and gain some downforce. The location is San Gabriel drag strip. (Bob Muravez.)

Due to pressure from his family, Bob Muravez was forced to retire from driving but continued to work as a crew member for the Special, now dubbed the "Freight Train." After an unsuccessful five-month-long search for a driver, Bob climbed back into the cockpit and promptly set a new NHRA Top Gas speed of 8.45 seconds elapsed time over 187 miles per hour. In order to hide Muravez's driving activity from his family, the team listed John Peters as the driver, and the Freight Train was back in the winner's circle taking home the Top Gas eliminator trophy at the 1963 NHRA Winternationals held at Pomona. In this image, the trophy is handed to a stand-in driver while Muravez stands in the background. John Peters is on the far right. (Bob Muravez.)

Here, Bob Muravez and the Freight Train take on the Buick-powered Frye Brothers car during first-round eliminations at the 1963 Winternationals. Not long after this, a pair of track announcers decided that Bob needed a "real" alias to drive under and dubbed him "Floyd Lippencotte Jr." In an unusual move, the NHRA issued Muravez an unlimited driver's license under the fictitious moniker. (Bob Muravez.)

Starting in June 1963 driving the Freight Train under his new alias, Muravez/Lippencotte Jr. toured nationally, winning the NHRA Springnationals in Bowling Green, Kentucky, in 1967 and Dallas, Texas, in 1969. The race depicted in this image took place in the late 1960s in Bristol, Tennessee, and was televised on the ABC Network show *Wide World of Sports*. (Bob Muravez.)

Muravez/Lippencotte Jr. and the Freight Train became hugely popular attractions at drag races around the country, drawing in crowds of as many as 30,000 people on a regular basis. At this US Dragster championship race at Lyons drag strip, Muravez and Peters are accepting a new sponsorship from M&H Racing tires. From left to right are John Peters; his wife, Beverly; Marvin Rifkin, owner of M&H; and Bob Muravez. (Bob Muravez.)

The year 1963 was a momentous one for the Road Kings of Burbank car club, with Don Prudhomme taking Top Fuel eliminator and Bob Muravez taking Top Gas. This shows Muravez and Peters as star attractions at the opening of the first NHRA supertrack, Orange County International Raceway, in 1967. (Bob Muravez.)

In 1966, at Lyons drag strip, Mickey Thompson staged an invitation-only race for drivers that had gone over 200 miles per hour. In what was the biggest event in drag racing to date, 117 Top Fuel dragsters went through seven rounds of elimination. Driving a new car owned by Don "the Beachcomber" Johnson, Bob Muravez was the top eliminator after winning all seven rounds. In this shot taken after the race, an exuberant Muravez gestures to his crewman John Seagraves as he is surrounded by a crowd that includes some of the biggest names in drag racing at the time. At far left is future world's land speed record holder Craig Breedlove, standing fourth from left is Johnson, and Thompson is fourth from the right, looking into the camera with a happy grin. (Bob Muravez.)

In 1965, Muravez/Lippencotte Jr. drove Nye Frank's nitro-fueled, twin-engine unblown Chevrolet-powered streamliner AA/fuel dragster "the Pulsator," pictured here, which won the Best Engineered Car award in the 1965 NHRA Winternationals at Pomona. (Bob Muravez.)

Bob Muravez retired from racing in 1971 and came back to drag racing in the early 1990s doing exhibition runs in the restored Freight Train. In 2015, Muravez was inducted into the International Drag Racing Hall of Fame. Here he is in 1964, at the height of his career, burning rubber at the place where it all began, San Fernando Raceway. (Bob Muravez.)

Like other members of the Road Kings, Bob Muravez's daily driver was something special. In the summer of 1954, Bob's father bought him a used Corvette as a reward for hard work. Purchased from Schoenlaw Chevrolet in Hollywood, this was not just any used 'Vette. Hand-built by Chevrolet as a developmental prototype, the Corvette was displayed at the 1953 Motorama car show, held at the Pan-Pacific Auditorium in Hollywood. It was then presented to film star Betty Grable by Chevrolet as part of a promotional deal. Grable owned the car for less than a year before trading it in, and soon, it fell into Muravez's hands. He replaced the automatic transmission with a three-speed manual and added some racing tires. He sold it a few years later, but the historical Corvette still exists and is worth over six figures. (Bob Muravez.)

After retiring from racing, Muravez continued to live in his hometown, Burbank, like most of his fellow members of the Road Kings. For many years, Muravez ran a successful business there and kept his hand in by building his own motorcycle. Buying a surplus Harley-Davidson motor trike from the Burbank Police Department, Muravez converted the former "meter-maid" trike into his daily driver. As seen here, Muravez (and his dog) were a common sight on the streets of Burbank in the 1970s. (Bob Muravez.)

Just north of the Valley in Newhall was Saugus Speedway. For 50 years, the one-third-mile oval track hosted midget racers, roadsters, and later, NASCAR stock car races, along with the occasional rodeo and circus. Road Kings member Dick Plamondon in the 209 car passes another Chevrolet in nighttime action at the track. The speedway closed in 1995 after the grandstands were condemned as unsafe. Like San Fernando, it is now the site of a weekly swap meet. (Dick Plamondon.)

Before joining the Road Kings, Dick Plamondon was a member of the Rod Busters, a club from the nearby beach town of Venice. Plamondon is kneeling third from left. Club president Ray "Red" Lewis stands second from left. While they did a little racing, the Rod Busters were primarily a social or cruising club. (Dick Plamondon.)

Two

On the Road

The Road Kings did not restrict their hot-rodding activities to the San Fernando Valley. One Saturday in the late 1940s, Don Hoffman and Jim Miles made a trip to El Mirage dry lakebed to do some speed runs. While they were there, a "weekend warrior" from the California Air National Guard decided to beat up the starting line in his P-51 Mustang, resulting in this dramatic image. Note the 1936 Cord 810 at lower left. It was owned and run by Don Montgomery, who went on to publish a famous series of pictorials about hot-rod history. His Cord was powered by a GMC inline six truck engine with an aluminum head and a Howard cam. (Don Hoffman.)

Road Kings members enjoyed many adventurous trips to drag strips throughout Central and Southern California. This was taken during an overnight trip to the strip at Inyokern, a several-hour drive from Burbank. (Tom Jandt.)

Club members Butch (left) and Dave Cederquist relax at Inyokern after the late-night drive. Their roadster can be seen on its trailer in the background, attached to the mildly customized black Ford F-100 pickup that the brothers used to tow their hot rod sporting spinner hub caps and wide whitewall tires. (Tom Jandt.)

Here is a daylight shot of the club at Inyokern, with the Cederquist brothers' roadster in the center. The white snap-brim caps seen on many of the members were considered to be very fashionable drag strip attire back in the 1950s and could be seen at strips up and down the West Coast. (Tom Jandt.)

Parked in the pit area of the drag strip at Inyokern, the deuce bakes in the desert sun. The Cederquist brothers' roadster is at right. The stock three-speed transmission that Ford used in its flathead V8-powered cars could not handle the higher output of more modern overhead engines like the Oldsmobile and would routinely self-destruct. The sturdier unit used in LaSalle cars of the late 1930s was the transmission of choice for most hot rodders. (Tom Jandt.)

Brothers Butch (in white hat) and Dave (in T-shirt) Cederquist stand by their trailered roadster early one morning in May 1957 at Inyokern drag strip before a day of racing. Tom Jandt's coupe can be seen in the background. (Tom Jandt.)

The famed Mondello and Matsuhara AA/fuel-altered Fiat and its Chevrolet C10 push truck wait in the pit area before a race at San Fernando. As seen in this early image from 1960, the Fiat body is colored a relatively quiet shade of metallic blue, rather than the garish striped paint scheme of later years. (Courtesy of Jim Campbell.)

"TV" Tommy Ivo (left) and Tom Jandt (right) are seen here in longshot as they strut confidently down the staging line at San Fernando. At the time this image was taken, around 1956, the two were undoubtedly the fastest drivers in the San Fernando Valley and Los Angeles County as well. (Tom Jandt.)

When Tom Jandt went to the races, he traveled in style, towing the coupe with his Ford Thunderbird. Jandt's rig is pictured here during a late-night road trip parked in front of the post office in the small desert town of Inyokern, California. (Tom Jandt.)

Tom Jandt would often make the long drive from Burbank to the drag races held at the Los Angeles County Fairgrounds. Here, the coupe can be seen parked behind a very cool customized Ford F-100 pickup truck. The "scalloped" paint job mimics that of the 1930s GeeBee racing planes. (Tom Jandt.)

A reputation for engine problems and other issues prevented the 1947 and 1948 Crosley from being a success with a little over 20,000 units sold. In later years, many of the surviving examples were used as the basis for drag racers, like the one at right in this image from May 1957. (Courtesy of Tom Jandt.)

In the autumn of 1957, a small group of Road Kings and their friends made the pilgrimage to the annual Speed Week held at Bonneville Salt Flats, Utah, to run club member George Calloway's 1934 Ford-bodied lake racer. From left to right are George Calloway, Gary Osborn, Ted Warbief, unidentified, and Ivan Umberson. (Tom Jandt.)

Tom Jandt caught the Denver-based Kenz and Leslie 777 streamliner on its trailer while at Speed Week. Seven years earlier, the twin flathead–powered streamliner was the first car to break 200 miles per hour at Bonneville with driver Willie Young behind the wheel. (Tom Jandt.)

This is the first version of the Linde Lakester. Powered by a Wayne-Chevrolet inline six in this image, the Lakester is still in existence, although much changed in appearance from what is seen here. (Tom Jandt.)

Few hot rods are as classic as the 1932 Ford roadster. Tom Jandt caught this neat example sitting in the pits at Bonneville. From its clean appearance, the rod has not been out on the salt flat yet. (Tom Jandt.)

Jandt also took this image of a pair of track marshals approaching the Calloway car for inspection under the hot sun of the Utah desert. The sun helmets they are wearing were common headgear during Speed Week. (Tom Jandt.)

Bonneville has always been a place of experimentation, especially in the early days. A wide variety of engine configurations and driver's positions were tried out to find out what worked and what did not. A lot of lake cars were built by people who were skilled mechanics but not trained engineers. As cars began to go faster and faster, fatal accidents due to mechanical failure increased, and safety regulations began to tighten up. Rear-engine cars like this Model T–bodied racer were banned from the dry lake by the 1960s. (Tom Jandt.)

The crew of this roadster has the luxury of a sunshade to work under and a tow truck equipped with a camper shell. For most participants of Speed Week, work was done out in the open under the blazing sun. Note the Chevrolet station wagons in the background. (Tom Jandt.)

Studebakers were a big presence at Bonneville during the late 1950s, with several individuals running cars and even the manufacturer getting involved at one point. Standing at far right with his foot on the bumper is Bonneville regular Belmont Sanchez, a tireless Studebaker promoter and the man responsible for what the contemporary motor press was calling "the Studebaker Revolution" at Bonneville. (Tom Jandt.)

Calloway built the radically chopped and modified lake racer with Ted Warbief and managed to reach 200 miles per hour on his run. Ted Warbief stands at left while a shirtless Calloway seems to be adjusting something on the racer's firewall. (Tom Jandt.)

The pale-blue coupe was particularly well finished and typical of the cars operated by Road Kings members. The arrow-shaped object at lower left that appears to be stuck into Calloway's thigh is actually the racer's push bar. (Tom Jandt.)

Tom Jandt and friend Ivan Umberson rode out to Utah in club member Gary Osborn's new Plymouth Belvedere sport coupe. While at the salt flats, they ran into a traveling pin-striper who offered to stripe Osborn's new car for a modest price. Here he is at work, the tools of his trade visible in the foreground. (Tom Jandt.)

The town nearest to the salt flats is Wendover, Utah, which back in the 1950s had relatively few places to stay. Lucky Speed Week attendees were able to get rooms at the air-conditioned Wendover Motel. Here, a group works away at their tank racer in the motel parking lot. At far right is a Chrysler engine sitting in the dirt. (Tom Jandt.)

Here, the Road Kings group sits in front of their rooms at the Wendover Motel. Calloway's lake racer and its tow truck sit at right. The motel's management took a very permissive stance on allowing guests to work on their cars in the parking lot. (Tom Jandt.)

The billboard at the entrance of the course was and still is a landmark to those in the racing community. Here is how it looked in 1957 as Gary Osborn poses in front of it with his new Plymouth. (Tom Jandt.)

Hot Rod magazine showed up at the 1957 Speed Week with its new 1958 Plymouth Fury Special. The highly modified factory demonstrator had just come from the speedway at Daytona, Florida, where it set a course record of 166 miles per hour. (Tom Jandt.)

It is mid-morning on the salt flats as the cars and drivers wait in line for their chance to run. A crowd is gathered around the streamliner at center, and George Calloway's 1934 coupe is visible in the left corner of the image. Note the narrow slit rear window on Calloway's car. (Tom Jandt.)

This image gives a good idea of the vastness of the desert racecourse, which can be seen running across the center. The couple sitting in this nicely turned-out Model T roadster seems to be working on their sun tans. (Tom Jandt.)

Here, in the open pit area at Bonneville, a mechanic works on the Ardun-Ford engine of this bodyless lake racer. What looks like a Crosley body sits on the ground at right, although it appears too small to fit onto the racer's frame. (Tom Jandt.)

One of many machine shops in North Hollywood that also dabbled in automotive performance was Frank Cannon Engineering, which had a shop located at Vineland Avenue and Chandler Boulevard. While Tom Jandt was at Bonneville, he managed to take a few snapshots of Cannon's black-and-white-painted lake racer. The driver sat in front of a fuel-injected 331-cubic-inch Chrysler Hemi. Note the aircraft-style clamshell canopy. (Both, Tom Jandt.)

Valley resident Clive Richardson's highly modified 1953 Studebaker Champion coupe is pictured here. The engine has been moved back into the middle of the frame, and Richardson drove the car from the back seat. (Tom Jandt.)

Various Speed Week attendees gather around the Studebaker while the Floating Mountain, a Bonneville landmark, looms in the background. In the foreground, a pair of mechanics mull over a headless Hemi block hanging from a chain above the salt flat. (Tom Jandt.)

Three

THE DRAG STRIP

Legal drag racing action in the Valley was done at San Fernando Raceway. Located in the west Valley town of San Fernando, the strip was operated by local businessmen Fritz Burns and Bill Hanna. Opened in 1955, the strip was on an unused airplane taxiway bordered on the north by an aqueduct and on the south by the San Fernando Airport. In this image from the strip's mid-1960s heyday, Road Kings founder Jim Miles in the Magic Muffler AA/fuel altered storms off the starting line. (Jim Miles.)

Before San Fernando Raceway opened, drag racing was done at Lou Baney's Saugus drag strip, in nearby Newhall. It was nothing more than an asphalt taxiway, with no bleachers, timing tower, or concession stand. (Tom Jandt.)

When it opened in 1955, San Fernando had all the amenities that Saugus lacked, like a tower and grandstand. Because of noise complaints from nearby housing developments, racing was restricted to Sundays from 9:00 a.m. to 3:30 p.m. Cars without mufflers could not race until 12:30, and the time trials, eliminations, and featured eight-car Top Fuel and Top Gas shows all had to be finished by 3:30 in the afternoon. In this shot, Rod Pepmuller leaves the starting line in the Road Kings club roadster. The timing tower is visible in the background. (Tom Jandt.)

Real estate developer Fritz Burns and businessman Bill Hanna teamed with county parole officer Darryl Morgan in a scheme to build a place that would attract local hot rodders off the street and onto a legal drag strip. (Tom Jandt.)

Early on, Morgan took a liking to a North Hollywood car club called the Road Rumblers. Soon, members of the club took on jobs like safety inspector and track marshal. Flagman Dave Cederquist (standing at left) was a Road Rumblers member who was also a Road King. (Tom Jandt.)

After a few years, Darryl Morgan left and the Road Rumblers' time as hosts of the strip ended, and Harry Hibbler took over as general manager and ran the track as a business. Hibbler is standing at center presenting a trophy to Road King Tom Jandt as film star Carolyn Craig looks on. (Tom Jandt.)

This image was taken at San Fernando before the sound wall in the background became covered in advertisements. That's Bart Chinchero of Burbank High School behind the wheel of his fully fendered 1932 roadster. (Tom Jandt.)

This unidentified dragster seen on a qualifying run at San Fernando is a good example of state-of-the-art in about 1960. Rails like the one pictured here were still relatively affordable to build and race and were becoming common at drag strips not only up and down the West Coast but also across the rest of the country as drag racing's popularity began to grow and crowds of race fans began to flock to the drag strip. (Tom Jandt.)

This black 1957 Chevrolet, which appears to be a 210 Del Ray club coupe, is spinning its wheels at the starting line as the flag starter (at far right) prepares to drop the green flag on what looks like a qualifying run. (Tom Jandt.)

This Chevrolet-powered twin-engine dragster made an appearance at San Fernando. The big machines put on a good show at the races, and the popularity of Ivo's dragster with spectators encouraged a lot of people to build their own. (Tom Jandt.)

Mechanics from Howards Racing Cams of Los Angeles were a common sight at drag strips up and down the California coast as well as at places like Bonneville Salt Flats and El Mirage dry lake. Here, two of them appear to be working on a twin-engine dragster at San Fernando. (Tom Jandt.)

The short wheelbase and light weight of fuel-altered cars combined with large, powerful engines could cause some unpredictable handling characteristics—usually bad ones. This Fiat-bodied example was run by the team of Reneke, Jackson, and Stern. (Tom Jandt.)

This Lincoln-powered dragster run by Ito's Automotive has an interesting front suspension arrangement. The drilled Ford front axle is supported by a transverse-mounted leaf spring, which is assisted by a pair of gas shock absorbers. The frame rails appear to be recycled from an actual passenger car frame rather than using welded tube. (Tom Jandt.)

While San Fernando drag strip offered spectators grandstand seating, many preferred to view the action from the chain-length fence that ran along the east side of the strip. On the right, the fenced-in pit area can just be seen. (Jim Campbell.)

The pits, as the staging area where dragsters are prepared for racing are known, are hallowed ground at any drag strip where only crew and drivers are allowed to enter. At San Fernando, the pits ran along Glenoaks Boulevard. (Jim Campbell.)

On a busy Sunday at San Fernando, the pits were a beehive of activity. This image shows a couple of GMC push/tow trucks, a pair of altered roadsters, and a Hemi-powered twin-engine dragster at center. (Jim Campbell.)

Drag racing pioneer Jim "Jazzy" Nelson of the Bakersfield Smokers car club visited San Fernando often. Driving a flathead-powered Fiat AA fueler, he was a regular crowd pleaser. Nelson would later design and build a monster of a twin-engine dragster called "The Outlaw." (Tom Jandt.)

Tony Monsoor, a neighbor of Norm Grabowski in nearby Sun Valley, put together this beautiful custom 1947 Mercury lowrider convertible. The early-style maroon custom sports a bobbed nose, frenched headlights, and a new grill. (Tom Jandt.)

The clean and simple interior of Monsoor's Mercury was finished in white vinyl. Visible in the upper-right corner is an accessory common in almost all customs of the day, a folding spotlight. Since there appears to be an aiming handle, this one may have been functional—many were not. (Tom Jandt.)

Floridian Don Garlits and the Don's Speed Shop "Iskenderian Special" paid a visit to San Fernando during Garlits's historic 1959 West Coast tour. "The Special," seen here in the pits minus its nose cone, had just set the world record for a gas-fueled dragster on January 4, 1959, at Santa Ana with a speed of 180 miles per hour with Garlits behind the wheel. It was sponsored by one of the biggest figures in the West Coast drag racing scene, camshaft manufacturer Ed Iskenderian. Iskenderian, whose cams were becoming famous for dramatically improving performance in racing engines, was also a shrewd businessman whose sponsorship of high-profile drivers like Garlits led to his company becoming one of the biggest names in speed equipment. (Tom Jandt.)

This shot is looking north, down the drag strip, with the aqueduct visible in the center background. The tower and grandstand are out of the picture to the right. Dave Cederquist is the flagman. Racing at San Fernando continued until 1970, when the strip closed for a variety of reasons, including complaints from nearby residential neighborhoods about the noise. The site is now used for a weekly swap meet and is also partially covered by a fast-food restaurant. (Don Hoffman.)

Flanking Tommy Ivo's T-bucket, unidentified members of the Road Kings watch as a roadster storms down the strip at Santa Ana in 1956. Almost all of the drag strips in Southern California are gone now, victims of rising real estate values and the nonstop expansion of residential neighborhoods. Drag racing has changed as well, and it is no longer possible for the amateur on a low budget to compete. But while some things have changed, others remain the same. The Road Kings are still active, and their car shows and other events that they sponsor attract thousands of people each year. Car culture and the hot rod lifestyle are still very much alive in the San Fernando Valley and will likely continue. (Tommy Ivo Collection.)